IMAGES OF ENGLAND

BUNGAY TO BECCLES
VOLUME II

IMAGES OF ENGLAND

BUNGAY TO BECCLES
VOLUME II

CHRIS AND TERRY REEVE

TEMPUS

Frontispiece: The once familiar clock tower atop the printing works of William Clowes – a landmark alongside the tall chimney, which could be seen for miles around the Waveney Valley until they disappeard in the early 1970s.

First published 2004

Tempus Publishing Limited
The Mill, Brimscombe Port,
Stroud, Gloucestershire, GL5 2QG
www.tempus-publishing.com

British Library Cataloguing in Publication Data.
A catalogue record for this book is available from the British Library.

ISBN 0 7524 3314 8

Typesetting and origination by Tempus Publishing Limited.
Printed in Great Britain.

Contents

Acknowledgements

The images for this book have been gleaned from a number of sources and without the help and co-operation of several people its production would not have been possible.

First we would like to mention Roy Link, of Beccles. Many photographs from his extensive collection appeared in the first edition and his ready help was greatly appreciated during the compilation of this book. It is with great sadness that we report that Roy died in November 2003 and we would like this edition to be in part a tribute to what he did to preserve historic images of Beccles. His widow has kindly allowed us to draw on his collection again this time and we extend our thanks and sympathy to her.

On the Bungay side the collection of Town Recorder, Frank Honeywood, has again proved an invaluable source. Over the years he has filled the role in a committed and dedicated way and has amassed a huge collection of material, so that the history of the town in photographs and other images is carefully preserved for future generations.

We are also indebted to both Beccles Museum and Bungay Museum for allowing the use of their collections, particularly Jimmy Woodrow and Keith Hibberd at Beccles for making the arrangements there.

Thanks also to: Colin Buck, who has an impressive collection of Mettingham photographs for such a small village; David Broome, of Gillingham Village Hall Committee; Bob Skinner, of the Chocolate Box at Bungay; Ron Walding, for material from the Clowes Printing Museum; All Hallows Hospital at Ditchingham, for use of their archive material; Shirley Stone, of Bungay, and Mrs D.M. Bloss, of Bungay; David and Christine Allen of Workingham and Ian Gosling of Bungay for the cover photograph.

Introduction

This is the second edition of images that look at the twin Waveney Valley towns of Beccles and Bungay, and their adjoining villages, in times past.

These are active communities with a wealth of history, many local organisations and many personalities, situated along the banks of the beautiful River Waveney on the Norfolk–Suffolk border.

The first edition, published six years ago, looked at some of the characters, the schools, shops, buildings, street scenes, the railways, floods and industry in general. In this edition there is some overlap of those topics, but we have endeavoured to find photographs to give a wider look at the people and activities that give the area its charm and appeal.

As a reminder, both towns are mentioned in Domesday book of 1086. Beccles is now the larger of the two, with a population of around 11,000, situated five miles to the east of Bungay, which has 5,000 inhabitants. Beccles is noted for its detached church tower in the town centre (the original tower slipped down the steep side of the valley centuries ago), its position on the edge of the Norfolk Broads, which gives it a significant number of water-borne tourists and its charter granted by Elizabeth I in 1584.

Beccles suffered a serious fire that destroyed many homes, shops and places of industry in 1586 and Bungay suffered an even worse fire just over a century later, in 1688. Over 400 buildings were destroyed or damaged and many people left homeless. Only about six buildings escaped entirely, but a national petition was raised which brought in £30,000 for the repair and renewal and it became a fashionable place in the eighteenth century. In both Beccles and Bungay, many of the finest buildings postdate those disastrous fires which inhabitants were largely helpless to contain.

Beccles was a borough for centuries and its council was, and still is, headed by a mayor, elected annually in May. The current mayor is Jack Walmsley.

Bungay has a castle, built by the Bigod family, who came over with the Norman Conquest; a fine common, Outney Common with an 18-hole golf course and its best known landmark is its domed Butter Cross in the Market Place.

It is also the only town in the country to retain the title of Town Reeve, an ancient office thought to date back to Saxon times. The Town Reeve heads the Bungay Town Trust, set up in 1639 and which from then until 1910 was Bungay's main administrative body. When the urban district council was formed in 1910 and took over that role, the town trust retained the town lands, the Butter Cross, the weekly market, the borough well, the town clock and almshouses in Outney Road. Since then it has acquired other almshouses in Staithe Close and the Castle Hills, in the town centre. Bungay also has a town council which, since 1997, has given its chairman the title of Town Mayor of Bungay. The current Town Reeve is Diana Belcher and the current Mayor, Susan Curtis.

For many years book printing has been the main industry in Beccles and Bungay and this book has a section on that – Beccles has William Clowes & Son, while Bungay has Clay's, formerly the Chaucer Press, that prints many high profile works, including the currently popular Harry Potter books. Both companies were established in the nineteenth century, both are still going strong and are among the biggest employers in the Waveney Valley, though at Beccles the plastic bottle industry, established much more recently and featuring two companies (M.&H. Plastics and Fibrenyle), employs more.

Two roads link the two towns. On the Suffolk side of the river Barsham, Shipmeadow and Mettingham stand between them and on the Norfolk side, Gillingham, Geldeston and Ellingham, while to the north and west of Bungay two other villages adjoin it, Ditchingham and Earsham. This book takes a look at those village communities, too.

There are many legends relating to the Waveney Valley, with the best known undoubtedly surrounding the Black Dog of Bungay. In August 1577, a fierce black dog dashed into St Mary's church during a violent thunderstorm and terrified the congregation. Several people were said to have been attacked and two men in the tower tolling the bell (to frighten away evil spirits, thought by some in those days to cause the storms) were killed on the spot.

This book also includes sections on local worthies, children, hospitals, transport, music and drama. The first edition proved very popular – we hope this one will prove equally so.

Chris and Terry Reeve
May 2004

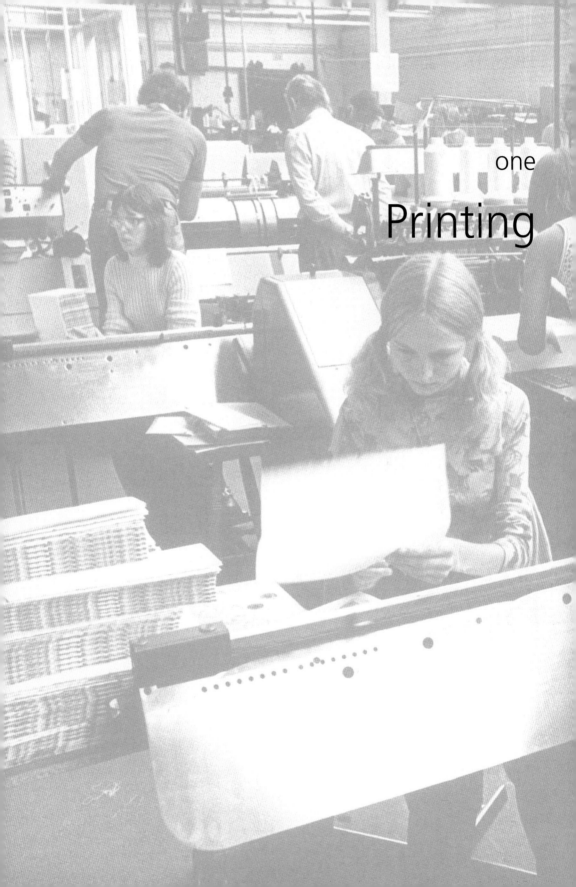

one

Printing

The Foundry at Clay's Printing Works in Bungay, around 1947/48. This was the department where plate-making took place. Those depicted, from left to right, are: Jack Winter; Leslie Stone Snr, (standing); Stanley Reiner; Peter Nice; Lenny Humphries (all seated towards the back); Bob Honeywood; Ted Hall; Ernie Beamish, standing, who, as can be seen, had an artificial arm due to injury during the First World War and Stanley Calver, seated, on the right.

A typical scene from the works at William Clowes at Beccles in the 1950s, as a battery of Heildeberg cylinder machines goes into action.

A ladies' tug-of-war event must have seemed decidedly risqué in the immediate post-Victorian period. But this team from one of the departments at Beccles printers William Clowes were clearly putting their best foot forward in this event from 1909, on the sports ground beside The Avenue.

The prize-giving was an important part of any sporting event, of course. This was the scene, around 1910, with the finely draped table set out with the prize silverware and Lady Beauchamp, in the large hat, presenting an award to one of the younger competitors to the right of the table. On the left, in the darker suit and beard, is Col. W. Wilson, then works manager at Clowes.

The works' social gathering was a traditional event in the first half of the twentieth century . Here employees of the Caxton Press enjoy their tea and social gathering, in the social club, on 2 October 1920.

Some of 'the gang' – the factory girls at William Clowes taking a break in the sunshine. This photograph was probably taken during or just after the Second World War.

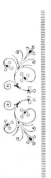
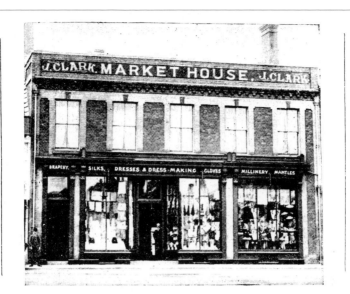

The above attractive premises occupy one of the best positions in Beccles, being situated at the upper end of the New Market Place, and visitors are at once struck with the commanding front and up-to-date appearance of the premises generally. Few ladies can resist the temptation to examine somewhat carefully the well-dressed windows, and, on being induced to step inside, are equally pleased with the variety, style, quality, and value of the stock of **GENERAL DRAPERY** placed at their disposal. Certain departments, however, evidently receive SPECIAL ATTENTION.

DRESSES.—J. CLARK'S special training and long experience in this department has secured a very large amount of support, and a striking and almost unlimited display of all kinds of **DRESS FABRICS** is the result, the **VALUE** being **UNRIVALLED THROUGHOUT.**

DRESS - MAKING is very successfully conducted on the premises under the personal superintendance of **MRS. CLARK**, and the utmost satisfaction is now guaranteed, **HIGH CLASS STYLE** and **WORK**, with **PERFECT FIT**, at **STRICTLY MODERATE CHARGES**, having been duly appreciated.

Mourning Orders receive prompt and very special attention.

JACKETS & MANTLES.—This department, in charge of **MISS ELLEN CLARK**, is one of the most successful and important, and to which great attention is devoted. A **VERY LARGE** and **FASHIONABLE STOCK** is always on hand, and arrangements exist whereby an assortment of any class of garment not in stock can be submitted within a few hours.

MILLINERY.—Under the management of **MISS EDITH CLARK** this attractive department has made rapid progress, **HIGH-CLASS EXCLUSIVE STYLES** at popular prices securing due appreciation. **MOURNING** Orders receive prompt and careful attention.

GLOVES.—Several makes are **SPECIALITIES** and cannot be obtained elsewhere, and an immense business is done in the **1/11½ KID GLOVE** alone, every pair being **ABSOLUTELY GUARANTEED**, an occasionally unsatisfactory pair being willingly exchanged. A very full assortment is kept in stook.

HOSIERY, FRILLINGS, LACES, RIBBONS, SILKS, VELVETS, FALL NETS, CORSETS, SKIRTS, FURS, TRIMMINGS, and **HABERDASHERY** are very fully represented; and remarkable value is being given in **FLANNELS, FLANNELETTES, SHIRTINGS, CALICOES, LINENS, SHEETINGS, QUILTS,** and **BLANKETS.**

J. Clark, at Market House, Beccles, was situated in New Market, in the vicinity of the present F.W. Woolworth store. It dealt in general drapery, dresses and dressmaking, hats, gloves, underwear and linen. It was clearly a family business with Mr Clark involved in the dress department, Mrs Clark looking after dressmaking, Miss Ellen Clark the jackets and mantles and Miss Edith Clark the hats.

Above: Beccles Caxton, or Caxton, was the name given to the social and sporting side of printers William Clowes' activities. Their football team – this was the one in 1920/21 – played at senior level for many years, mainly in the East Anglian League.

Left: Two members of the staff of William Clowes at Beccles at work under the old hot metal system.

Athletics was another sport in which William Clowes staff were active in the pre-war and immediate post-war period. This photograph is of the Caxton Athletics Club men's and women's team from around 1950.

...and the cricket team from a similar period, in a varied collection of sweaters and caps.

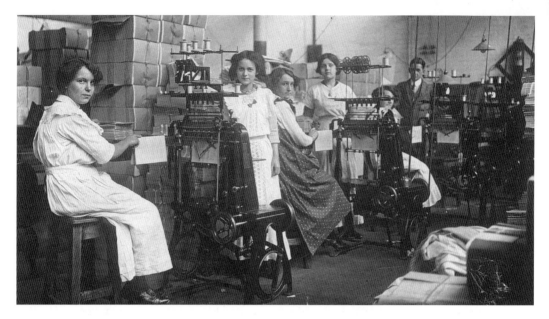

This was the scene in the bindery department at The Chaucer Press, now Clay's of Bungay, around the time of the First World War, when women were employed in the task of stitching books. The large piles of packaged books can be seen clearly on the left. The workers are photographed from left to right: Elsie Kent; Maggie Love; Flo Mayes; Jessie Knights and Elsie Johnson. The name of the man at the back, possibly the department supervisor, is not known.

These girls are photographed at work in the book-sewing section of Beccles printers William Clowes, c. 1960. The machines they are working on in the foreground are the semi-automatic Brehmer machines, then an up-to-date development for the factory.

WALTER J. COPEMAN,

FAMILY BUTCHER,

NORTHGATE ST., BECCLES.

BEEF, MUTTON, AND PORK,

Of the Best Quality at Reasonable Prices.

Corned Beef, Pickled Tongues, Home-Cured Hams & Breasts.

VEAL AND LAMB IN SEASON.

Home - Made Sausages and Lard.

FAMILIES WAITED UPON DAILY.

⊰ SMITH'S ⊱

Commercial and Temperance Hotel

AND

Dining Rooms,

STATION ROAD,

BECCLES.

Pleasure Parties catered for.

Accommodation for 150 persons.

ORDINARY, 1 p.m.

There would have been many shops in Northgate, Beccles in the early part of the twentieth century. This advertisement from an East Anglian Health and Holiday Resorts brochure, printed by Beccles printers William Clowes, around 1920, shows that Walter J. Copeman was a butcher there and the sort of quality products he offered. The other advertisement is for Smith's Commercial and Temperance Hotel which was situated in Station Road.

Above: One of the specialist items printed by William Clowes of Beccles – a Bible little larger than a box of Swan Vestas matches, probably from the 1930s.

Left: A part of Beccles industrial scene in the first half of the twentieth century including the Victorian water tower and chimney at South Road, photographed in 1949. They were later demolished to make way for housing.

two

Children

Above and left: With the beautiful River Waveney running through Bungay, Beccles and their local villages, generations of children in the Waveney Valley learned to swim in the river – in fact, Bungay Primary School took children for swimming lessons at Sandy, a popular swimming hole on Bungay Common, where hundreds of people of all ages would gather on hot summer days to bathe. There were a number of such swimming places – this one was known as Poplars, because of the poplar tree that grew beside the river, until it blew down. These two photographs from 1947 show groups enjoying the sunshine and the water there – it was a place for boys to meet girls. Photographed sitting on the fallen poplar tree are, from left to right: Eddie Sampson; Win Southgate; Hazel Brighton; Pat Buck and Jenny and Bobby Savill.

Eager children turn round for the camera at Gillingham Village Hall, before tucking into the food at the Christmas party, c. 1954. There were plenty of them there to enjoy it and with the vicar clearly in attendance, it may have been the Sunday School party.

All children are arrayed in fancy dress for the festivities in Gillingham for the Coronation of Queen Elizabeth II in 1953. Plenty of creative imagination in these costumes, but who would pick a winner?

Children playing in the road in Mettingham, in the early part of the twentieth century. In the background, on the left, is the Tally Ho public house, still a popular venue for drinks and food today. The tower of Mettingham church can be glimpsed through the trees.

Two boys in Staithe Road, Bungay, c. 1860. This very early photograph depicts the old 'pound' on the left, which was used for impounding stray animals. Staithe Road has changed enormously since this photograph was taken and is now largely a residential area. The poverty of many families in the Victorian period is indicated by the boys' ragged clothes.

Scouts and Sunday School children depicted outside the Wesleyan Methodist Chapel in Trinity Street, Bungay, in the early years of the twentieth century. The minister, standing towards the back of the group and wearing a white flower buttonhole, was Mr Chapman. The children were probably gathered together for a special Sunday School event, perhaps an excursion or picnic.

Bungay Boy Scouts, photographed in 1914/15. The clergyman seated in the centre of the photograph is Canon Hawtrey Enraght, who was the vicar of Holy Trinity church from 1913–22. This photograph may have been taken in the rectory garden. The boy in the foreground is clutching the Scouts' standards and the boys standing in the second row are holding their band's musical instruments.

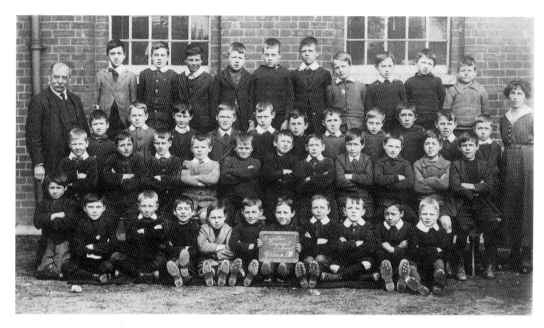

Here are the boys of Beccles Council School, around 1910, with their teachers. In those days, of course, boys and girls were segregated. Note the very visible soles of the hobnail boots of the boys sitting in the front row.

And these are the girls at the same school, which was probably the Peddar's Lane School at Beccles, around ten years later (*c.* 1920). Ribbons and Alice bands in the hair were clearly in fashion then.

These children are photographed outside their Beccles school, *c.* 1910. It is probably Ravensmere School, today one of the smallest in Suffolk and what is unusual about it is that the children are photographed with toys – a dolls' house and a toy milk barrow can clearly be seen on either side in the photograph.

This group is photographed outside the main entrance of what was Bungay Area School, later Bungay Secondary Modern school and now Bungay Middle School, in 1947. The twenty-two photographed were all aged about thirteen.

The 'bonny baby' show was a popular event at fêtes and fairs, particularly in pre-war days. These proud mothers are seen at The Pavilion at Valley House, Mettingham, at an event marking the Silver Jubilee of King George V and Queen Mary. Like their mums, most were wearing the fashionable headgear of the day.

All ready for the fancy dress at one of the village fêtes or other occasions – this is Betty Belorgy and Colin Buck at Mettingham in 1939. By the look of it Betty is a gipsy and Colin a jockey.

This photograph was taken in the yard to the rear of the Swan public house in Bungay. The yard was quite regularly used for entertainments in the nineteenth and early twentieth century and here children are enjoying playing on the swings that may have been set up in connection with some celebration in the town. The Swan is situated near the market place and is one of Bungay's oldest pubs. Its name has recently been changed to Swanson's.

Children, in fancy dress, at the Bungay Carnival in 1926. This was a major event for the town and other photographs depict the massive crowds that assembled to see the carnival procession and other displays taking place.

Empire Day celebrations at the Beccles National School, which was in Peddar's Lane, in 1907.

All along the Waveney Valley fishing was – and still is – a favourite pastime for young boys. This group is seen in the 1950s at Beccles. Roach, dace, bream, perch, carp, sand gudgeon and eels were among fish excitedly hauled out by successive generations of amateur anglers.

three

Music and Drama

A scene from one of the many lavish productions staged by the Beccles Caxton Amateur Operatic Society in pre-war and post-war years. This was probably the cast of the February 1932 production of *A Slave in Araby*, a two-act comic opera, produced by Mr L.E. Watson. The musical director, Mr Waldemar Schapiro, is photographed (right of centre) in a bow tie.

Members of the Bungay Mutual Improvement Society taking part in a theatrical performance in May 1907. In this photograph they are performing a dialogue entitled *Wonderful Bungay*, which may have been inspired by the song of *Old Bungay*, performed at the town's theatre in 1816, in which every verse concludes with the chorus: 'Oh, what a town is old Bungay, Old Bungay's a wonderful town'.

Right: Christmas and the Nativity Play, was a regular seasonal celebration in the Beccles and Bungay area, as elsewhere. This was the scene at All Saints church, Mettingham, around 1953, as young members of the church re-create the nativity. Among them are Cecily Meen, as one of the wise men, standing behind Mary (Jennifer Knights) and Glynis Castleton, the angel kneeling on the right. The angel at the back is Audrey Knights.

Below: This group of children was taking part in a Mettingham church play, *c.* 1924. Ivy Meen is standing on the left, Kathryn Mills second from the right and Peggy Tilney on the right, while those sitting or lying on the grass mount include, on the left, Muriel Meen and next to her, Dot Meen.

This wonderful photograph, taken in 1908, depicts all the people involved as vividly as if it had been taken yesterday and is a tribute to the photographers of the Edwardian period. The event was a dramatic recreation of Bungay history in the grounds of the castle, organised by the Bungay branch of the Friends of Waifs and Strays.

The secretary of the organisation was Maude Maddle a headmistress at the St Mary's School and the text of the performance was written by Mr J.O. Kemp. Many well-known Bungay families were involved in the production, including the Wightmans, Hartcups, Normans, Chases, Nurseys and Clays.

The Beccles Light Symphony Orchestra, which provided the music for many productions in the town. Their director, Mr Waldemar Schapiro, is photographed standing at the back in the centre. This photograph was featured in the programme for the Beccles Caxton Amateur Operatic Society's 1932 production.

The Women's Institute in rural villages has always been strong, ever since the movement was founded. This photograph shows a group who took part in a Gillingham WI production, around 1928, when clearly a lot of effort went into costumes. Photographed in the back row are, from left to right: May Mayston; Mrs Peck; Peggy Spall; Ada Thrower and Cathy Thrower. Front, from left to right, are: May Spall; Mrs Hemmant; Mrs Stimpson and Mrs Hemmant's dog, Toby.

For the **BENEFIT** of
Mr. **S T A C K W O O D** and Mr. **C O U R T N E Y.**

N E W   T H E A T R E   B U N G A Y.

On Thurfday June 5 1794. the much Admir'd Comedy Call'd

ALL in the WRONG,

OR, AN ENDEAVOUR,

TO BE ALL RIGHT AT LAST.

Sir John Reftlefs,   **Mr. F I S H E R**
Beverly,   **Mr. P R A T T**
Sir William Belmont,   **Mr. S T A C K W O O D**
Young Belmont,   **Mr. C O U R T N E Y**
Mr. Blandford, Mr. **P A S T O N** --- Robert, Mr. **W O R T H I N G T O N**
Bruth,   **Mr. M A L L I N S O N**

Lady Reftlefs,   **Mrs. F I S H E R**
Belinda,   Mifs **J E S S U P**
Clariffa,   Mifs **H O W A R D**
Tattle, Mrs.   **S E L L E E** --- Tippet, Mrs. **S C R A G G S**

After which A Favorite Mufical Entertainment Call'd the

Wedding   Ring; Or,

THE OBSTINATE LOVER.

Pandolpho,   Mr. **P A S T O N**
Henrico,   Mr. **W O R T H I N G T O N**
Zerbino,   Mr. **F I S H E R**

Felicia,   Mrs. **F I S H E R**
Lifetta,   Mrs. **S C R A G G S**

To Which will be Added (Never Perform'd Here) A D I A L O G U E On

E N G L I S H AND F R E N C H.

F R E E D O M.

Jack Oakum,   Mr. **F I S H E R**
French Jacobin,   Mr. **P R A T T**
Sailors, &c. by the reft of the Company.

To Conclude with RULE BRITANNIA, in full Chorus.

✝✝✝ No admittance Behind the Scenes on any Account.

Tickets and Places to be had of **Mr. J. Dyball**, in the Market Place of
Mr **STACKWOOD**, at **Mr. R. ABLETT'S** and of **Mr. COURTNEY** at
the Widow **GIRLING'S, Erfnam Street.**

Poster from the New Theatre, Bungay, Thursday 5 June 1794. The New Theatre was
established by Nathaniel Godbold, in the Castle Yard and opened for its first performance
in June 1773. Subsequently, David Fisher became the proprietor and his company of actors
regularly performed there. Play performances became increasingly popular in the early part
of the nineteenth century, encouraging Fisher to provide a number of new theatres in the
larger towns of Norfolk and Suffolk. These included one in Broad Street, Bungay, which
superseded Godbold's building and became known as the 'new' New Theatre and later, as the
Fisher Theatre. It finally closed in 1844 and the building was used for other purposes – but has
recently been acquired by the Bungay Arts and Theatre Society who have reopened it for use
as a performing arts venue again. The theatre poster depicted here represents an element of
British jingoism – the *Dialogue on English and French Freedom* was probably influenced by the
blood bath of the French Revolution in 1789 and the programme ended with an enthusiastic
full chorus of *Rule Britannia*.

CORN HALL, BUNGAY.

GOOD FRIDAY, APRIL 15, 1892.

PROGRAMME.

MARCH		"Golden Trumpets"		*Dr. Fowles.*
QUARTETT		.."Rock of Ages" ..		*C. Buxton Grundy.*
SONG		.."The Chorister"		
		Miss M. Brown.		
DUET		"The Wings of the Dove"		*.. Michael Watson.*
		Mr. and Mrs. Sturgess.		
SONG		"At the Eastern Gate"		*.. Berthold Tours.*
		Miss Botwright.		
CHORUS		"The Starry Throne"		*.. Handel.*

CANTATA "A Daughter of Moab" Isaac Andrew.

PART I. - In Exile.

PART II. - Home Again.

PART III. - The Harvest Field.

PART IV. - The Harvest Home.

PERSONS REPRESENTED:

RUTH—Mrs. W. Sturgess.   NAOMI—Miss Sturgess.

ORPAH—Miss Debenham.   BOAZ—Mr. C. C. Botwright.

REAPERS, GLEANERS, A SERVANT, &c.

CONCLUDING CHORUS   "Gloria"   ..   ..   .. *Mozart.*

Above: A company of actors raising money for the Norfolk and Norwich Hospital. The title on the reverse of the photograph is 'Lantern Parade, 1893'. As all the performers are men (the 'lady' on the right is a man wearing a mask) they are probably members of a sporting association and the collecting box held by the Harlequin figure on the left bears the initials B.A.C., which perhaps stands for the Bungay Athletic Club. This photograph was taken by Benjamin Clarke who had a photographer's studio in Earsham Street, Bungay, between 1891–1922.

Left: When the Fisher Theatre closed in 1844, it was used as a Corn Hall, but concerts and other musical events still took place there. This programme was for a concert of religious music on Good Friday 15 April 1892.

Joining the church choir was a natural progression of going to Sunday School, which many children did in the first half of the twentieth century. This photograph of the choir of All Saints church, Mettingham, taken in about 1954, shows some of those who did just that. They include, in the front row: Michael Daniels (second from the left); Paul Leeder (third left) and Glynis Castleton (fourth left).

Ten Little Nigger Boys, part of a concert performed in Mettingham Village Hall in the 1950s. The boys, from left to right are: Lea Bird; Leslie Smith; Harry Turner; Charlie Boast; D. Brighton; Frank Eastaugh; Alfred Sampson; Peter Turner; Stanley Norman and Eric Belorgy. The owner of the photograph, Colin Buck, recalls that, as they sang the line, 'Ten little nigger boys, sitting on a wall', each boy in turn popped down below the curtain until they had all disappeared and then, at the end, they all popped up again. In those guises, probably not even their own mothers recognised them.

𝕭𝖚𝖓𝖌𝖆𝖞 𝕱𝖊𝖘𝖙𝖎𝖛𝖆𝖑 𝕻𝖆𝖌𝖊𝖆𝖓𝖙
1951

July 4th, 7.30 p.m.   July 7th, 2.30 and 7.30 p.m.

PRESENTED BY

𝕿𝖍𝖊 𝕮𝖎𝖙𝖎𝖟𝖊𝖓𝖘 𝖔𝖋 𝕭𝖚𝖓𝖌𝖆𝖞

ON

BUNGAY CASTLE HILLS

Extract from speech by His Majesty the King at the opening of the Festival of Britain :—

" I have been told of the pageants and displays which have been prepared in our ancient cities and throughout the country side. I congratulate most warmly all those who will help to make our history live before us and thus to send us forward with faith in our future."

The programme cover of the Bungay Festival Pageant held on 4 and 7 July 1951. The event took place on the Castle Hills and the drawing depicts Bidod's Castle as it appeared when it was first built in *c.* 1165. The pageant re-enacted scenes from Bungay's history from prehistoric times until the nineteenth century, concluding with a 'Grand Finale by the Fishers' Famous Company of Players'.

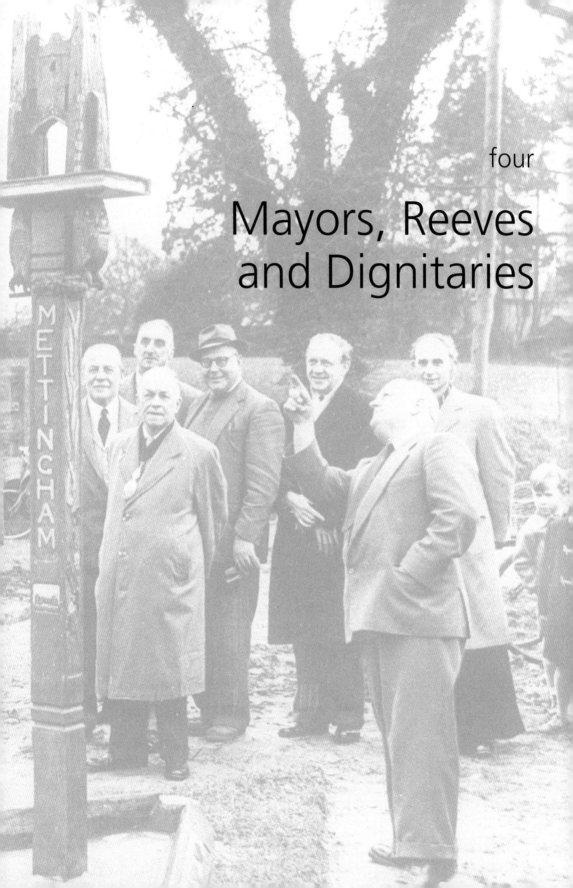

four

Mayors, Reeves and Dignitaries

The erection of the village sign at Mettingham, *c.* 1960. The sign depicts the gatehouse of Mettingham Castle, built for Sir John de Norwich in 1342. The dignitaries who have gathered for the unveiling include Conservative MP for the region, the Rt Hon. James Prior, standing immediately to the left of the sign. Next to him are Wilfred Sutton, Bungay Town Reeve 1954–55 and Cecil Harris, wearing the chain of office for Bungay Urban District Council of which he was Chairman from 1959–61. He became Town Reeve of Bungay, 1962–63.

Sir Alec Douglas Hume, Prime Minister, in Bungay on 16 April 1964 during a Conservative election campaign. He is addressing the crowds assembled around the historic Butter Cross. Pupils of St Mary's School and members of the Bungay Sea Scouts can be seen gathered around the platform. Two local doctors, Hugh Cane and Wyndham Jordan, can be glimpsed beneath the Butter Cross.

Above left: William Hartcup (1814–95) of Upland Hall, on the Flixton Road near Bungay. This photograph was taken in the gardens of his house in September 1885. He was articled to the Bungay legal firm of Kingsbury & Margitson in 1833 and succeeded to the entire business in 1848. A Justice of the Peace for Suffolk, he served as Town Reeve of Bungay for three periods of office. In 1893, on the occasion of their Golden Wedding Anniversary, he and his wife were presented with a beautiful silver candelabrum by the inhabitants of the town. This was later donated to the town by the Hartcup family and is regularly used at the annual town dinner.

Above right: Dr George Colborne, Town Reeve of Bungay, during the outbreak of the First World War. He was educated at Bungay Grammar School and following his medical training, became Medical Officer of Health for Bungay Urban District Council. He was presented with a silver chain of office for the Town Reeve's medal to replace the blue ribbon that had previously been worn.

Left: Horace James Inwards, Town Reeve of Bungay 1929–30. He opened the bakery in St Mary's Street in 1908, a business that later included confectionary and a tea room and flourished for more than fifty years. On his last day as town reeve Horace officiated at the opening of the town's new fire station that had been built by the Town Trust.

The proclamation of the accession of King George VI in Bungay Market Place in 1936. The proclamation is being read by Guy Sprake who had been appointed Town Reeve only a few days before this event. The accession of George VI followed the abdication of his brother, Edward VIII. In commemoration of the coronation, the Town Reeve raised money for a children's playground in Jubilee Road. In the background of the photograph can be seen the old Bungay Post Office, which moved to its present site in Earsham Street in 1940.

Dr Hugh Cane, Town Reeve in 1957–58. During his year of office he had this hanging sign made to direct visitors from the Market Place to the Norman castle just off the town centre, but hidden from sight. Dr Cane's father had been responsible for the renovation of the castle in 1934 and Hugh later became the castle's curator and organised further improvements.

General Election Day in Bungay in 1906. The local Liberal candidate, Sir Edward Beauchamp, has arrived in the town in his splendid motor vehicle to persuade Bungay people to vote in his favour. The smartly dressed lady in the rear of the car must be Lady Beauchamp. This photograph includes an array of electioneering posters on the wall of a building in Earsham Street and the premises have been taken over by the Liberals for use as Beauchamp's Committee Rooms. The slogans on the posters include: Keep the Flag Flying over Freedom, Untaxed Food, Beauchamp This Time and details of How the Tories have Increased the Cost of Living.

The Licensed Victuallers' Dinner at the Chaucer Institute in 1967. In 1967 the Town Reeve was Reginald McDaniel and he can be seen standing at the top table, fifth from the left. Paul Woodcock, town reeve in 1984–85 and his wife are standing third and fourth from the left next to Mr McDaniel. For many years Paul Woodcock was the manager of Peter Dominic's wine-shop in Broad Street, which is now Thresher's Wine Shop.

The official opening of the Oddfellows Centenary Rooms in Chaucer Street, Bungay, 17 May 1911. The building was designed in a mock-Tudor style, popular in the town in the late nineteenth to early twentieth century. The council chamber in Broad Street was built in a similar design. Among those depicted in the front row are: W. Cocks, the Lodge Treasurer (on the left) and Dr C. Ramsbottom, the Lodge Surgeon (fourth from left).

Mr Albert Pye was the Mayor of Beccles from 1952–54, a member of the borough council for many years and a great servant and benefactor of the community. In these two photographs he is seen in the mayoral robes and chain of office after being elected (left) and several years later in 1968, with other dignitaries, talking to children at the opening of the school that perpetuates his name in the town – Albert Pye Primary School (below). He died three months later

Pearle Elizabeth Taylor was the first woman Mayor of Beccles in the centuries-old history of the office. She held the title, as head of the borough council, from 1960–62 and is seen here on the left with other VIPs, after opening the 'Our Town Exhibition' in the town. She is admiring a fireman's helmet, an exhibit from the town's museum.

The Mayor of Beccles and part of his corporation photographed in the town on a horse-drawn landau. Mr Dawson Crisp Smith, Mayor in 1929–30, is photographed on the left with his wife, while on the right is James Brindy, who was the previous Mayor, in 1927–29.

Mayors were, of course, among guests of honour at all main events. This ceremony at Beccles in 1929 was attended by the then mayor, Mr Dawson Crisp Smith, who can be seen on the dais wearing his chain of office. He was attending the ceremony to receive and bless a brand new vehicle for the Beccles Home Ambulance Service. The man in the wig is the town clerk, Mr Bryan Forward.

David Frost is now a television personality of world renown and is the son of Revd Paradine Frost, Methodist Minister at Beccles for a number of years. David went to the Sir John Leman Grammar School and after becoming famous revisited the town on a number of occasions. Here he is speaking at the school's prize-giving in 1977.

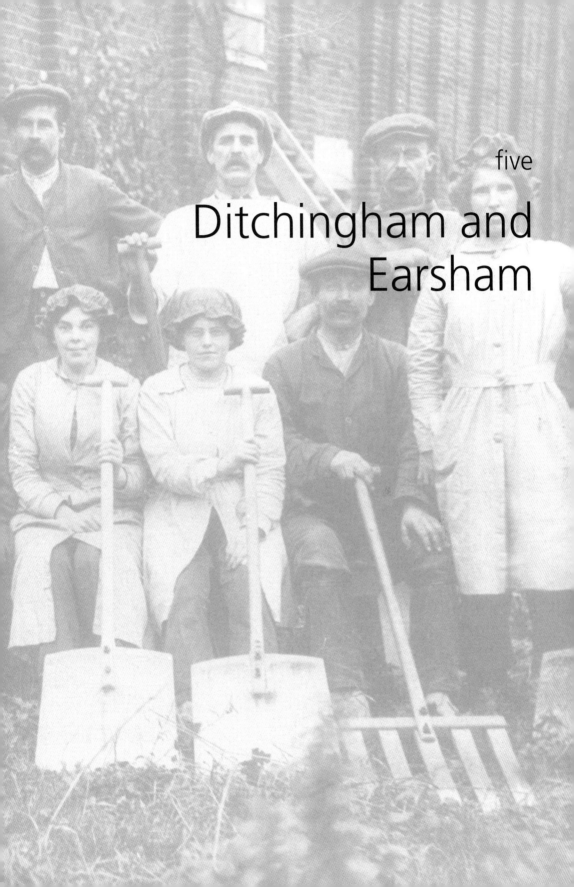

five

Ditchingham and Earsham

Above left: Doris Whiteland, *née* James, seated at Ditchingham Station in the 1930s. Mrs Whiteland was employed at Bungay Station during the Second World War.

Above right: Ditchingham Station, with the Signalman, Edward Kerridge, standing in the Signal-Box, *c.* 1930.

Ditchingham Railway Station in the 1930s. This aerial view depicts the steam train speeding into the station. The railway track from Bungay to Beccles, via Ditchingham was opened in 1863 when the Waveney Valley line was finally incorporated into the Great Eastern Railway network providing much speedier transport for local people. With the increasing popularity of bus and car transport after the Second World War, railway travel declined. The Bungay to Ditchingham line was closed in 1964 and the Ditchingham to Beccles line in 1965.

Wainford Maltings. This photograph from the 1920s depicts the employees posing with the tools of their trade including the large maltsters' shovels. Back row, from left to right: Sam Honeywood; Ben Bird; 'Shiver' Osborne; Jack Howlett; Pip Honeywood; –?– Laura Brighton. Seated, from left to right: Emily Snowling; –?–; –?–; –?–; Miss Mickleburgh (later Mrs Smith); –?–, Kelly Hindle. The smartly dressed man with the tie and watch-chain must be one of the owner-managers. The maltings had closed by around 1970 and the malting buildings were demolished in 1977.

Wainford Maltings, *c.* 1970. A family are enjoying some angling near the buildings and Mill House.

Above: The Bath House, Ditchingham, around 1900, viewed from Outney Common, Bungay. In the eighteenth century a spa was established on the site and it became a popular resort for the gentry and visitors to the region. The Bath House itself was an inn providing accommodation for guests. The Spa closed by around 1800 and the property was later acquired by Lady Haggard, widow of the author, Sir Henry Rider Haggard, whose estate it joined. It was inhabited by her daughter, Lilias Rider Haggard, in the mid-twentieth century and continues in use as a private residence.

Left: Ditchingham church, photographed by Thomas Smith, who had a shop and photographic studio at No. 3, Earsham Street, Bungay, *c.* 1890. His son, William, was also a photographer. This photograph, from around 1900, was reproduced from one of his old glass negatives.

This postcard, Souvenir of Ditchingham, has the stamped date of 28 November 1906. The small photographs feature, in the top row, from left to right: The Game-keeper's Cottage by the Waveney; Ditchingham church; the Windmill; Ditchingham Hall. Second row, from left to right: Ditchingham Dam; the River Waveney; Railway Station. Bottom row, from left to right: All Hallows Convent and Hospital and Ditchingham House. The River Waveney separates Bungay in Suffolk, from Ditchingham in Norfolk.

Pirnough church, near Ditchingham. This tranquil scene dates back to the early years of the twentieth century. The church, with its attractive patterns of flintwork, was closed for worship by around 1980. It was situated not far from Ditchingham Station and the gates connected with the railway can be seen on the right in the photograph.

SOUVENIR OF EARSHAM NORFOLK.

Above: This postcard, Souvenir of Earsham, was dated 7 November 1907. Postcards were becoming increasingly popular in the early twentieth century and this one depicts eight views of the village. Earsham is only a mile or so from Bungay. In the last century, before most families could afford to buy cars, the customary Sunday afternoon occupation was to go for a stroll around the villages. Walks to Earsham and a stroll along the river by The Wold were very popular and a longer walk, the Homersfield Round, included the villages of Homersfield and Flixton, as well as Earsham.

Left: Earsham church from a postcard dated 24 September 1906. The church is dedicated to All Saints and stands on an old encampment dating back to Saxon times. The fourteenth-century tower has a distinctive pencil-shaped spire, making it an easily recognisable landmark in the low-lying Waveney Valley.

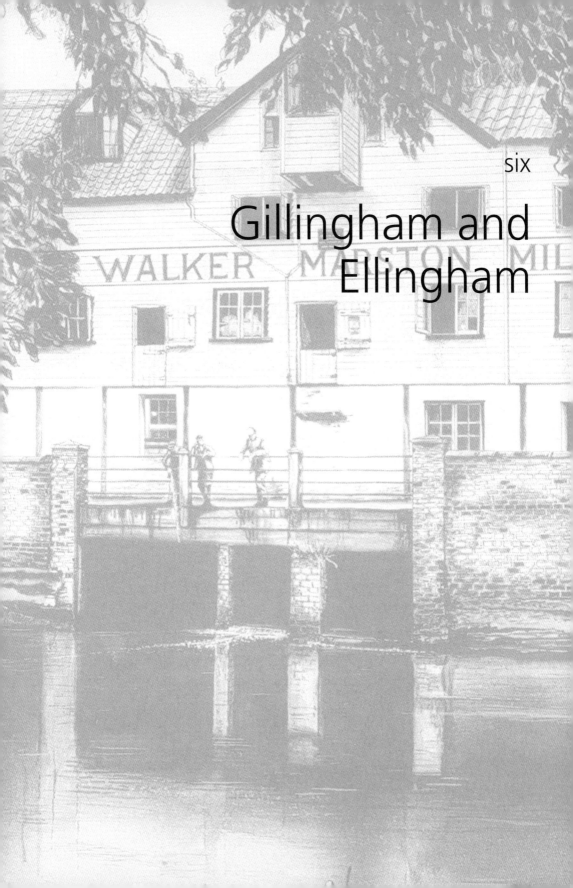

six

Gillingham and Ellingham

Above: J. Hawes' farm at Gillingham was an arable and pastoral enterprise, a family business enduring from well back into the nineteenth century. This photograph was taken around 1920 as four farm workers harvested potatoes by hand – in those days a painstaking task using forks, panniers and boxes.

Left: Dick Gray was a well-known character in Gillingham – and was probably considered a worthy there because of the work he did and help he provided for the community. This photograph is of the corner of Gillingham Street and Loddon Road in the early 1950s.

The Kawa Tea Gardens at Gillingham, enjoyed a certain amount of fame during the period they were operating, between 1915–1930. They were situated near the site of what was known as the 'House on the Marsh', towards Beccles, and could be reached by boat or on foot for those wanting to enjoy tea outside in good weather in peaceful surroundings by the river.

This is group three at Gillingham School, around 1910, when laced boots were very much the fashion and may well have been the only pair of footwear these children owned, with smocks the order of the day for the girls.

The village school at Gillingham stood on the corner of The Street and Gillingham Dam. This photograph, from around 1920, shows children on their way to the school, which can be seen on the right. Clearly there were no school uniforms in those days.

The Women's Physical Culture Movement was strong both before and after the Second World War. This photograph shows the ladies of the Gillingham and District Physical Culture Club at one of their meetings at the village hall in 1948. The seated lady fourth from the left is Miss Chaplin, who was a teacher at Gillingham Infant School, on her left is Mrs Hawes, who was a leading light in organising the club. The others photographed are, in the back row, from left to right: Dorothy Sheppard; Gwen Cubit; Frances Sparkes; Betty Feavyour; Muriel Hawes; Mrs Catchpole; Daphne Grimson; Ann Feavyour; Kathleen Norman; Mrs Nelson and Betty Hawes. Front, from left to right: Mary Burroughs; Viola Double; Brenda Goldsmith; Miss Chaplin; Mrs Hawes; Silvia Kemp; Grace Feavyour and June Grimson.

The men of Gillingham also enjoyed physical culture, probably on a more aggressive level. This photograph shows the senior and junior members of the Gillingham and District Physical Culture and Boxing Club (men) at the village hall in 1948. In the back row, from left to right, are: Baydon Pipe; George Dack; Billy Nelson; George Dowishe; -?-; Billy Pipe; Gerald Hinsley; Owen Case; Mr Curtis; -?-; -?- and Mr G. Cook. Middle row, from left to right, are: Leslie Cockrell; John Sutton; Ray Catchpole; Basil Thrower; Sir Charles Lloyd; Alan Darby; Leslie Mason; Bert Nelson and Johnny Pipe. Front row, from left to right, are: Dennis Thrower; Noel Green.; -?-; David Green; Dougie Cockrell; Alan Feavyour; Daniel Goldsmith; John Goldsmith; -?-; Larry Peck; Dennis Westgate; ? Nelson; Geoffrey Pipe and Wally Thrower.

Gillingham Dam, which links the village with Beccles, was flooded following the great downpour of August 1912. This photograph was taken on 28 August 1912, and while the couple in the boat seem to be on a summer's afternoon row, the two in the horse and trap seem to be in some difficulty!

This scene on the railway line between Beccles and Bungay, just beyond Gillingham, is from 28 August 1912 when phenomenal summer floods brought scenes like this throughout the Waveney Valley.

Ellingham Hall, from an early 1883 photograph. Children are playing around the garden seat on the right and on the left two gardeners are mowing the lawn. Ellingham has been occupied since Roman times and a Roman kiln and Saxon urns have been found near the hall and church.

This drawing is of Ellingham Mill, owned, as can be seen from the sign, by Walker and Marston, who also had a mill at Earsham and a maltings at Bungay. No doubt local wheat was ground here, powered by the waters of the River Waveney. The mill closed many years ago and it is now the private home of artist Margaret Thomas and is considered as a picturesque landmark on a byroad between Bungay and Beccles.

This photograph nicely captures three different forms of transport in one scene in The Street, Gillingham, c. 1900.

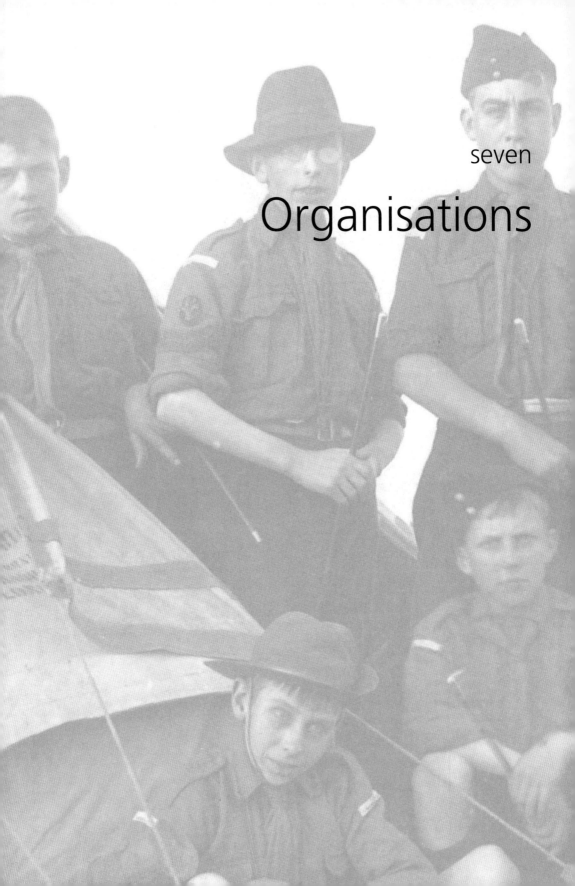

seven

Organisations

The Bungay First Company of Girl Guides, photographed in April 1920. Iris Reeve, née Ottaway, mother of the authors of this book, is depicted in the front row, third from left. She was aged twelve at the time and, later on, in the 1930s became the captain of another Bungay Guides Company.

Beccles and Bungay each had several football teams in the early years of the twentieth century, as the game grew in popularity. This was the team of St Julians FC at Beccles, photographed in 1912/13.

The Beccles and District Cage Bird Society is one of the town's older organisations. It was still going strong until recent years and this photograph was taken around 1930, at one of its trophy presentation evenings. The birds can be seen in their cages in the background. Mrs Ives, a stalwart of the society in those days, is seated on the left, with Mr Ives standing behind her. Beside her is Eva Allen, with Hubert Allen standing, third from the right.

Above: The Beccles Accordion Club was another popular group in the town. Members gave concerts and also played together for the fun of it, as well as taking part in Beccles activities. This was their float in the Beccles Regatta carnival parade in the early 1950s, with the image of a huge accordion dominating the trailer.

Opposite above: These are the ladies of Beccles Mothers' Union, photographed with the Revd Birch, who was Rector of Beccles from 1934–45. This photograph was probably taken just before the outbreak of the Second World War, in a period when the Mothers' Union movement was particularly strong.

Opposite below: This celebration was to mark the dedication of the banner of the Mettingham church branch of the Mothers' Union, *c.* 1954. The Bishop of Dunwich, on the left, dedicated the impressive banner, at a service at the church, assisted by the Minister at Mettingham, the Revd Hills, who can be seen on the right.

68

Above: The Beccles Social Institute is one of the town's most enduring organisations. It had several sections and its bowls section still has teams in the local bowls league today. This photograph, from the 1920s, shows members of the institutes St John's Ambulance section.

Opposite above: The Henham Harriers, who hunt hares, were established on the Earl of Stradbroke's Henham Estate in the late seventeenth or early eighteenth century and have met regularly ever since. Today they are known as the Waveney Harriers and their Boxing Day meet at Bungay, when the riders take their stirrup cup outside the King's Head Hotel in Earsham Street, has become a popular spectacle over the years, with crowds of up to 1,000 turning out to watch. They then move off to hunt in the Mettingham area. This photograph was taken at Mettingham, probably in the 1920s, with the church and the Tally Ho! pub in the background.

Opposite below: This is the Beccles patrol of the Incorporated Church Scouts, photographed during their annual camp at Lowestoft in 1913. Standing, from left to right, are: Fisk; Andrews; Gooch and Ling. Sitting, from left to right, are: Meadows; Knights; Peachey and Hammond (just out of shot).

The men of the Beccles Fire Brigade as it was in the 1890s, with highly polished helmets and buttons and the manual pump with which they tackled blazes in the town. The manual pumps in both of these pictures would have been drawn by horses. It may be that the Beccles brigade had both pumps at the same time.

eight

All Hallows and Hospitals

A view of All Hallows School soon after it was built, showing some of the girls working in the garden.

The Community of All Hallows at Ditchingham had three main elements to it at its height: the convent, the base for the religious community; the hospital and the school. This is one of the earliest photographs of the school, from around 1890, and shows some of the nuns, including Revd Mother Lavinia, with pupils in front of the original building.

This photograph was taken four years later, in 1894, with a group of girls from the school in front of the convent entrance. The range of headgear is interesting and some are holding tennis rackets, others croquet mallets and some musical instruments. Sister Constance is in the centre of the photograph.

All Hallows School, Ditchingham Playing Field

Sport was encouraged among the girls at the school. Here, some are playing hockey with the convent building in the background, *c.* 1911.

Another photograph from a series taken in 1911 showing pupils and staff – many of whom were nuns from the All Hallows Community – at the school.

The neat and tidy refectory of All Hallows School, Ditchingham, as it looked in 1911.

A much more recent photograph of young novices at All Hallows Convent preparing to take part in a summer festival procession.

The Convent of St Michael's and All Hallows was established at Ditchingham by Lavinia Crosse in 1855 and is photographed here, around 1890, across the arable fields of the village where farming was then the main livelihood. The daughter of a Norwich surgeon, Lavinia became the convent's first Mother Superior.

All Hallows Hospital at Ditchingham was set up in a cottage by Mother Lavinia in 1872.
A year later it opened on its present site in what is now Station Road. In this photograph,
taken in 1892, the name can be seen above the entrance – All Hallows Country Hospital. The
hospital can still be seen today.

The gentleman in this horse-drawn carriage outside the entrance to All Hallows Hospital is
Mr Codling, who had some connection with the nunnery. Perhaps he was a surgeon – until
relatively recent years minor operations were carried out at the hospital, where there were also
maternity facilities. This photograph is, around 1905.

All smiles as nuns and nurses receive gifts brought in for the annual Harvest Festival at All Hallows Hospital, c. 1960. A sheaf of wheat, flowers, fruit and vegetables are being delivered by members of the Ditchingham village community.

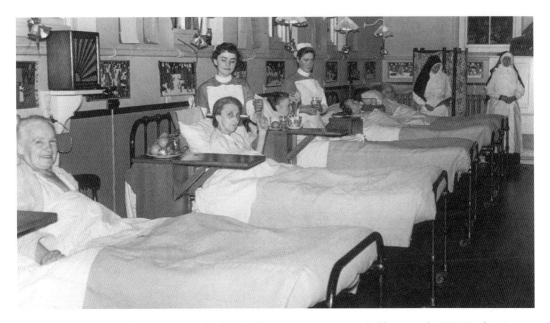

The scene in the ladies' ward at the hospital in post-war years, probably around 1955. By this time nurses, who were not nuns, had joined the staff caring for the sick at All Hallows.

This is the first hospital to be built in Beccles. It was erected in 1854 in Fairs Close, and the word Hospital can be seen carved along the front of it. It remained the town's hospital for many years, eventually being replaced by the War Memorial Hospital in St Mary's Road, soon after the First World War.

The Beccles War Memorial Hospital was officially opened on 16 February 1924 and built by public subscription on land give by Mr Alex Elliott. Dr Woodhill was the first GP to administer to the patients in the original twenty-four beds there. He is seen in this photograph of the opening ceremony, along with the Mayor of Beccles, Mr John Quinton Wilkinson, who held the office from 1923–25.

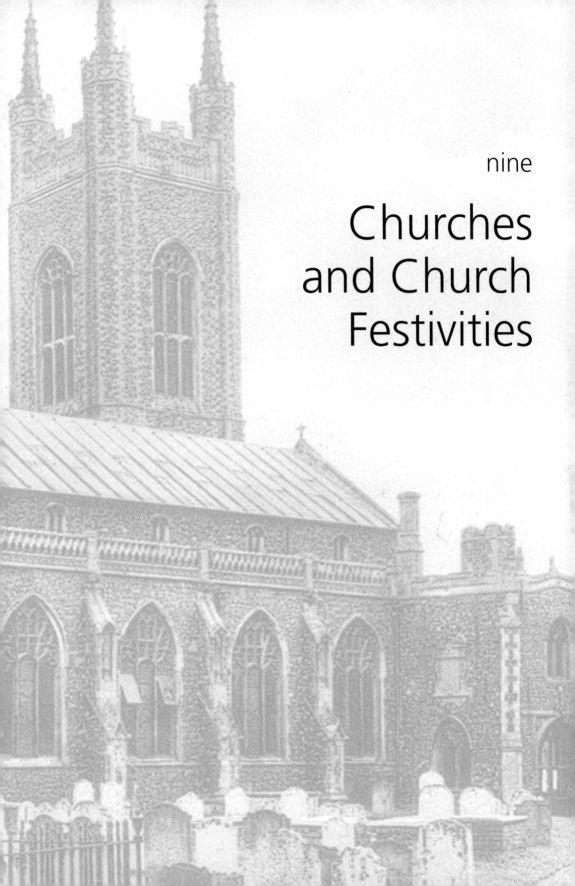

nine

Churches
and Church
Festivities

The interior of St Mary's church, Bungay, 1958. Canon W. Lummis is seated in the centre of the second row, surrounded by members of the choir and the church wardens. On the far left is Mr 'Lew' Roberts, the church organist and in the back row standing to the right of the Cross is Thomas

Foyster a choir member who, for many years, sang the song of *Old Bungay* at the annual Town Reeve's dinner. The choir stalls and other areas of the church have been decorated with flowers and fruit for the annual Harvest Festival.

The same event as above, depicting the entire interior of St Mary's decorated for the Harvest Festival in 1958. It was decided to close the church for regular worship in 1977 and it is now cared for by the Churches Conservation Trust. It was their decision to remove the curtains behind the altar, thus allowing the Victorian stonework with Biblical texts to be revealed. Flower Festivals, concerts and other events are still regularly organised in the church by the Friends of St Mary's.

St Mary's church, Bungay, from a postcard from, *c.* 1910. This is the north side of the church, dating from the fourteenth/fifteenth century, with some fine mediaeval gargoyles. During the Great Fire of 1688 much of the church was severely damaged but the north side was relatively unharmed.

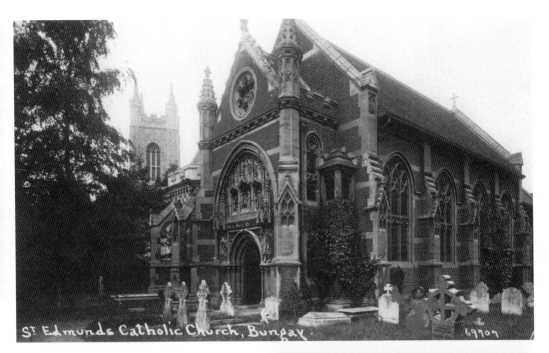

St Edmunds Catholic Church, Bungay.   69707

Above: St Edmund's Catholic church, Bungay, from a postcard of the 1950s. The church was built in 1823. Towards the end of the nineteenth century, Frederick Smith, a local solicitor, financed the rebuilding of the church and the elaborate façade, depicting scenes from the life of Saint Edmund, was added. He was also responsible for the building of the large Baptistry to the rear and rebuilding and improving the Catholic School close by. The tower of St Mary's can be seen to the left.

Right: The interior of St Edmund's Catholic church, Bungay, depicting the elaborately decorated font. The postcard perhaps dates from the First World War. It has a message on the back recording that the sender has just arrived in Bungay and expects to arrive 'at Saxmundham tomorrow morning at 9. 20 for Bath like the other Boys did'. The message suggests that he was in an army regiment and moving around the region. The card bears a halfpenny stamp, but there is no posting date.

Bungay Congregational chapel, from a postcard dated 6 May 1905. The Independent Congregational Community built their first chapel in Bungay in 1699. The building was enlarged in the eighteenth century. By 1976 the Congregational group had united with the Presbyterians and Methodists to form a United Reformed Congregation, all worshipping in the same building, which was renamed the Emmanuel church. The Emmaus room now replaces the front porch and the railings have been replaced by a low wall surrounding the attractive flower garden and burial grounds.

Holy Trinity church, Bungay, from a postcard from around 1950. The photographer was standing in the grounds of Trinity House, opposite the church and the flower borders of the garden can be seen in the foreground. As Bungay had two Anglican churches, within a short distance from each other, it was decided in 1977 that St Mary's should close and Holy Trinity became the sole Anglican church for regular worship.

Look carefully and you can see Mr Money, the Mayor of Beccles from 1908-10, looking out from the clock dial on Beccles church tower. Other members of the borough council are also in the photograph at different points. This was probably an event marking the mounting of the now-familiar town clock in its lofty position.

The tower of St Michael's church, Beccles, viewed from the Market Place, c. 1910. The bell-tower is detached from the church itself and was completed in the mid-sixteenth century. A plaque on the side of the tower records: 'With this Beccles Penny of 1795, the sixteenth century Tower was bought for Beccles in 1972'. During 2003, after substantial repairs had been completed, the tower was opened as a Tourist Information Centre.

The bell-ringers gotch, belonging to St Michael's church, Beccles. The gotch is dated 1827 and would be filled with beer and passed round from one bell-ringer to another when they had completed a ringing session, which could be very thirsty work. The incised inscription records that the gotch was the gift of John (Battman) of Beccles and the verses advise the ringers, 'Don't drink too much to cloud your knobs, Or you'll forget to make the bobs'. (Link, Brown album No. 5)

FLIXTON CHURCH.

St Mary's church, Flixton, a postcard from around 1905. The church was founded in Saxon times and rebuilt in the Medieval period. It was considerably altered in the Victorian period when the tower was taken down and a new one built in the unusual style depicted here.

The Waveney Valley has a number of Saxon round-towered churches, with the towers dating back to the tenth and eleventh centuries. This is typical of them – it is the church of All Saints, South Elmham, near Bungay.

Above: The Castle is one of Bungay's most important historic buildings and it became marketed as a tourist attraction in the early 1900s. Here it is depicted on the left in this Souvenir of Bungay postcard, dated 3 September 1906. At this time the walls were overgrown with ivy and the site occupied by chickens and brambles, but in 1935 the town reeve, Dr Leonard Cane, organised extensive clearing and renovation work. The three town centre churches are also depicted.

Left: The twin towers of Bungay Castle Gatehouse photographed in the snow by Bill Wright, *c.* 1960. The lofty tower of St Mary's church appears in the background. The castle keep is now a ruin but when it was first built, in the twelfth century, it is thought that it would have been even taller than the church.

ten

Transport

Above: The old and the new – nineteenth-century horse-power is depicted alongside twentieth-century motor-power. The manager and staff of the Beccles & Bungay Co-operative Society were clearly proud of their new van that stands in the centre of the photograph, while the firm's horse and cart is at the rear. The van bears the hand-painted advertisement: Beccles Co-operative Society Steam Bakers. This photograph was taken in Earsham Street, Bungay, *c.* 1910.

Opposite above: Bungay's first fire station was situated in Cross Street, near the Market Place. A new, purpose-built fire station was built on the site of the former Wharton Almshouses in Lower Olland Street and opened in December 1930. Here, a crowd of boys and adults have assembled to see the firemen set off to deal with a fire; the postcard is dated Saturday 10 August 1935.

Opposite below: A charming photograph of three smartly dressed girls with their bicycles and the sun filtering through the delicate tracery of the leaves in The Avenue, Beccles, *c.* 1900.

The Avenue, Beccles.

Above: The donkey and cart was a fashionable form of conveyance in the Victorian and Edwardian periods. It is not known where this photograph was taken, but, judging from their costume, the children are clearly from a wealthy family.

Left: This horse and cart with the home-made tarpaulin covering makes an unusual sight in the streets of Bungay, *c.* 1970. The couple depicted may have been attending the Barsham Fayre, which was a popular annual event in the 1970s, featuring folk music and dancing, crafts and all kinds of entertainment. Many people camped out on the Barsham church field for the weekend.

Beccles is connected with the Norfolk Broads waterways; a very popular area for holidaymakers. This photograph, taken in 1907, depicts a group of yachtsmen on their craft *Cybele*. Bungay, the other market town in this area, was also connected to the Broads by the River Waveney, but by the 1920s the river had silted up and is now only negotiable for rowing-boats and canoes.

On the right is the steam ship *Jean Hope*, used for towing lighters up the River Waveney near Beccles. The photograph was taken in the early part of the twentieth century.

Bungay Fire Brigade, with the horse-drawn cart that provided the transport for both the men and their fire-fighting equipment. However, in this photograph, it has been decorated, probably as part of the town's celebrations for Queen Victoria's Diamond Jubilee in 1897. This photograph was taken on the old Recreation Ground near Earsham Dam.

The fire station building in Cross Street, Bungay, where the fire-fighters' cart and equipment was kept. The keys were kept by a fireman in Trinity Street and the horses were grazed on the common, so there must have been some considerable delay before any fires could be dealt with.

These cars and lorries, lined up in Bungay Market Place in 1932, bear banners promoting Bungay Baby Week. It was part of a national government initiative to promote the health of mothers and children and Bungay Museum has a plaque presented to the organisers who set up a baby-welfare centre in the town. Mothers with their children in prams are depicted on the right and the banners bear slogans including: Better Babies; Brighter Bungay, and Healthy Babies, Happy Homes.

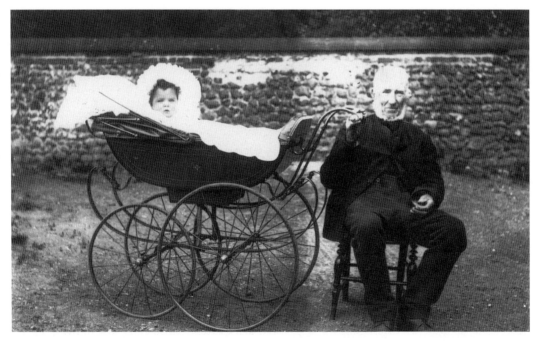

This photograph was taken around 1890, in the Bungay district. It depicts a smartly dressed baby in a splendid perambulator. The wheels appear to be iron-framed without tyres, so baby must have had rather a bumpy ride on the rough paths and roads of the period.

The threshing machine used at Earsham Hall Farm, *c.* 1930. Earsham is just across the river from Bungay, in Norfolk. Men and boys are assisting with building the stack, right.

A 'break for four'ses'. The workers and horse at Earsham Hall Farm pause in their work to have a photograph taken before enjoying a well-earned break.

A Bungay postboy, with his delivery bike, *c.* 1900. About twenty-six staff were employed at the Market Place Post Office and a later photograph, from around 1910, depicts four Royal Mail delivery carts and four postmen and boys with bicycles.

Bingham's butcher's shop was situated in Earsham Street, Bungay, in the last century and closed around 1955 when the business was taken over by Ramm's. The slaughterhouse was situated to the rear of the premises, backing on to Bungay Castle. Like most butcher's shops of the period the interior had the walls covered with white ceramic tiles to create a clean and hygienic appearance. This photograph was taken around 1920 and depicts one of the shop girls posing on her delivery bike, with the meat basket on the rear, advertising: F.W. Bingham, Butcher, Bungay.

The shop premises of Harry W. Woods in Bridge Street, Bungay. Mr Woods was a collar, saddle and harness maker and the photograph shows a variety of the goods he sold displayed in the shop window, including dog-collars, stirrups and grooming brushes. His workshop would have been situated to the rear of the premises. Mr Woods had a prosperous trade in the period, around 1900, when horses were still the main form of transport.

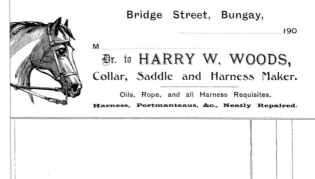

Bridge Street, Bungay,

190

M

Dr. to **HARRY W. WOODS,**

Collar, Saddle and Harness Maker.

Oils, Rope, and all Harness Requisites.

Harness, Portmanteaus, &c., Neatly Repaired.

A piece of the headed note-paper, from around 1900, used by Harry W. Woods in connection with his saddlery business.

An excursion organised by the Great Eastern Railway Company on their transport buses. The scene depicts Loddon Plain and it seems that the bus on the left is heading for Norwich and that on the right, for Beccles. The date is around 1900, when most towns and several villages in the area were connected with the Waveney Valley Railway line.

Above: A bus, parked by the Butter Cross in Bungay, *c.* 1934. The driver and the ticket collector, wearing pale coloured coats, are standing near the vehicle and the smartly dressed family nearby are maybe waiting to alight the vehicle, destined for Lowestoft via Geldeston and Beccles. Public transport by bus became increasingly popular in the 1930s and 1940s, as it was generally cheaper than a train journey and could convey passengers closer to their destinations. As a result, several railway passenger stations in the Waveney area were forced to close in the 1950s including the Bungay Station in 1953.

Opposite above: Employees of Watney, Combe Reid & Co. in Bungay posing for the photographer before setting off on their first annual outing in July, 1920. Most of the men depicted were maltsters, or employed in other jobs at the brewery, including wherrymen and lorry drivers. The manager Mr D.E. Beckett is seated in the centre of the front row, sixth from the left, with his assistant manager Mr Blye, fifth from the left and the brewery's clerk, Mr Newby, fourth from the left. In the background is one of the brewery's lorries used for the staff outing, which no doubt would include a pint or two of ale at one of the region's pubs.

Opposite below: Horses and carts lined up outside Crowfoot's Brewery at Ditchingham. The beer barrels can be seen piled on the carts ready for delivery. The small, independent brewery flourished between 1880 and 1910. Brewing and public houses suffered a decline during the First World War, because the majority of men were away fighting and new licensing laws restricted the sale of alcohol.

Cameron's Ironworks was situated in Earsham Street, Bungay, and was a prosperous business throughout the nineteenth and early twentieth century . Here, the employees are lined up with the tools of their trade to the right and in the centre of the photograph is the delivery cart bearing the firm's name. In the foreground is one of the ploughs, which was one of their most successful products. On the left is Daniel Cameron, owner/manager and the man holding the bike is Harry Rumsby who later succeeded to the business.

J. Lambert & Sons of Ditchingham had a slaughterhouse business and the lorry depicted must have been one of their vehicles for transporting cattle and other animals to the abattoir. The driver posed beside his vehicle is Mr James and the photograph was taken in the 1930s.

Steam lorries were part of the commercial scene for many years, after the invention of the internal combustion engine. This one was being operated by Green's Flour from its Castle Mills in Beccles in the 1920s.

Horses and carts remained the main form of transport for many years after the invention of the motor car – the one here was also owned by Green's. With George Keable at the reins, it is photographed on the meadow at the rear of the flour mill, which was in the area of what is now Castle Hill, around 1920, loaded with sacks of flour.

A boating party on the River Waveney near Outney Common, *c.* 1900. Boats could be hired from the Kings Arms public house which stood near the river in Bridge Street. Later on, in the 1920s–30s, George Baldry, author of *The Rabbit Skin Cap*, hired boats from his cottage to the common at Ditchingham.

In this picture from around 1910, the building in the background is probably the maltings at the bottom of Station Road, Beccles, but the large cogwheel being carried on the horse-drawn cart suggests it and the driver are probably in the employ of the town's iron foundry, Elliott & Garrood, in nearby Gosford Road.

Robinson's Garage, in Newgate, Beccles, was one of the first in the town to deal with cars, as well as bicycles and prams. This photograph was taken in the 1920s and features the workforce, with Mr J.W. Baker, who lived at Mutford, standing third from the right and Hubert Allen, third from the left.

The Lowestoft-registered steam drifter SD Consolation, photographed at Beccles, *c.* 1920. Boats used to bring herring up the Waveney to Beccles from the seaport, but it is thought this one was there for work to be carried out on it by Elliott and Garrood, the town's foundry.

Happy days, when the only vehicle to be seen in Broad Street, Bungay was a horse and cart slowly wending its way towards the Market Place. That was, *c.* 1920. Today, since Bridge Street was made one way for motor traffic in 2003, Broad Street has become the main road for vehicles entering the town from the Ditchingham direction causing much annoyance for local residents.

Cycling became very fashionable in the late nineteenth century. It was popular with both sexes and for the first time, allowed young women the freedom to travel about independently, without family chaperones. The long skirts worn by these ladies, around 1900, could not have been ideal cycling wear, as they could easily have become entangled in the bicycle chains. The photograph seems to have been taken near the walls of Bungay Castle.

eleven

The Wars and Military Events

Above: Men from the Bungay Regiment of the Norfolk Volunteers, photographed in the early 1900s. This photograph may have been taken on the old Recreation Ground, near Earsham Dam. The band sergeant, W. Honeywood, is standing on the right.

Left: This studio photograph depicts band sergeant W. Honeywood with the Ladies' Challenge Cup. It was presented to him by the ladies of Bungay in 1908 in recognition of his fortieth year of service with the Volunteers and Territorial Forces.

Band - Sergt. Honeywood,
Winner of the Ladies' Challenge Cup, 1908
in his fortieth year of service with
the Volunteers and Territorial forces.

Above: Another photograph of the Bungay Volunteers Band members at their camp site, *c.* 1900. The men are depicted holding their musical instruments and Mr W. Honeywood, later the band sergeant, is depicted in the centre of the back row. The band was often used to provide the music for ceremonial events in Bungay.

Right: Colonel Herbert James Hartcup (1844–1914), was born in Ditchingham and lived in the Bank House in Broad Street following his marriage in 1875. He joined the Volunteer Force in 1863 and later became a colonel, commanding the 2nd Voluntary Battalion of the Norfolk Regiment. He was a Town Reeve of Bungay for seven periods of office and died in May 1914, only a few months before the outbreak of the First World War.

Army troops engaged in training exercises on Bungay Common, during the First World War. Soon after war was declared, large numbers of soldiers were billeted over a wide area of Outney Common, because it provided an ideal wide-open space for practising their manoeuvres. The common was normally used as an area for grazing cattle and for recreational activities such as golf, angling, football and the annual races. All these activities had to cease until the war was over.

Another photograph of troops in training on Outney Common. In May, 1916, 1,800 men from the 62nd West Riding Division of the Royal Engineers arrived in Bungay and took over the golf club building as their officers' mess. They also took over public halls in the town and a canteen for their use was provided in the St Mary's Mission Hall in Broad Street, quite close to the Common.

Although the Second World War ended in May 1945, all young men continued to be recruited for the forces in case further warfare ensued. This photograph was taken in around 1947 and depicts the No. 4 Company, Bungay 3rd Cadet Battalion of the Suffolk Regiment. They are practising their drilling and manoeuvres at Beccles.

The drummers and band of the same regiment as depicted above.

Bungay volunteers lined up with their bikes, around 1890, during the Boer War. This photograph was taken on the recreation ground near Earsham Dam, a site regularly used for football matches and other sporting events.

This photograph was taken in East Anglia on 17 June 1917. During the First World War the threat of German Zeppelin attacks was ever-present. The Suffolk coast, not far from the Waveney area, was one of the first places to suffer an air raid and on 15 April 1915, German airships dropped their load of bombs on Lowestoft and Southwold. During the summer of 1916 more bombs were dropped during Zeppelin raids on Bungay Common and the recreation ground near Earsham Dam.

The Mettingham and Ilketshall St Andrew Home Guard during the Second World War. The men are grouped outside Bungay Castle. Bungay Museum has a similar photograph of the Bungay Home Guard in 1944. On 3 December 1944 the stand-down parade of all Home Guard units took place and a photographer was hired to take photographs at the castle of the three local groups.

The Bungay Cadet Battalion on parade outside their regiment headquarters in Nethergate Street, Bungay. They are being inspected by their officers on the left and a group of children has gathered to watch.

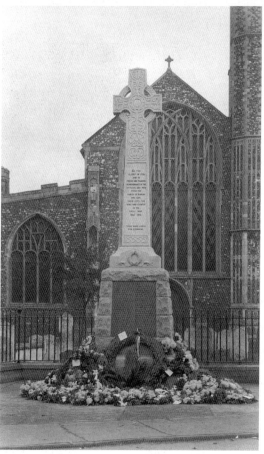

Above: The scene here is at the Beccles War memorial in St Mary's Road on 1 October 1919, as a monument to those from the town who died in the First World War, was unveiled. As can be seen, a large crowd gathered, many of them grieving for sons lost, and a bugler is ready to play the last post and reveille.

Left: The War Memorial outside St Mary's churchyard was unveiled on Sunday 13 November 1921. It records the names of all the 101 officers and men of Bungay who died fighting during the First World War. This postcard was probably made not long after the memorial was erected. A Remembrance Day service is still held annually in November at St Mary's church and wreaths of poppies are laid at the Memorial, similar to some of those shown here.

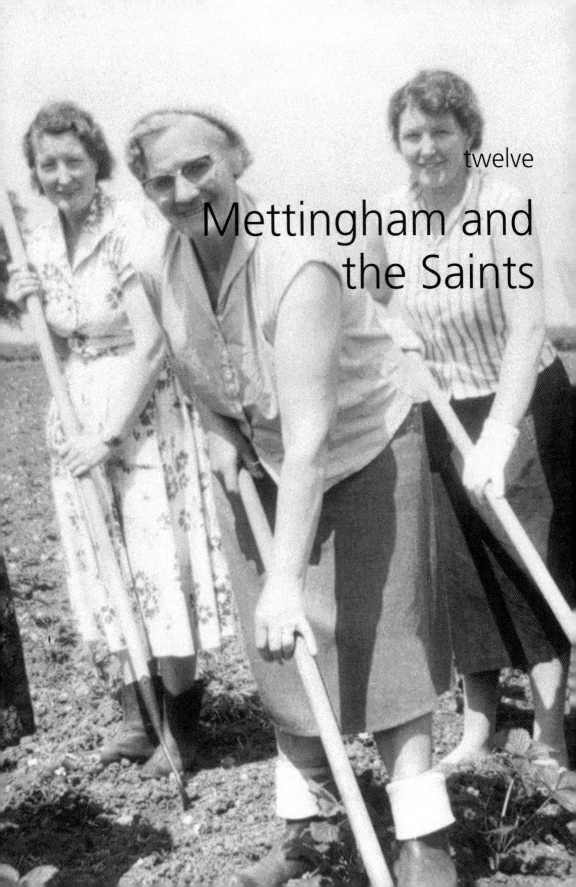

twelve

Mettingham and
the Saints

The road between Bungay and Beccles has changed much over the last fifty years. Watch House Hill is the steepest part of it, as you leave Bungay and move into Mettingham. This is what it used to be like, around 1955, before road widening work made it safer for the increasing volume of traffic.

Having got up the hill and down the gentler incline beyond, you come to the Tally Ho! pub. This is what the road used to look like then, around 1955, when the road ran close to the pub – it is now the parking area in front of it – before the pub was modernized. The Austin car belonged to Leman Smith.

Robert Tilney was the village postman at Mettingham, but as money was needed to keep the family Robert, like so many, took on other work when it was going. Here he is hoeing sugar beet at one of the local farms in the 1920s.

Strawberry plants at Red House farm, Mettingham, also had to be hoed to keep them free of weeds. Here a team of women are photographed tackling the job, with Elsie Hart, second from the right and Mrs Read, on the right.

Another part of the year's work at Castle Farm, Mettingham, owned at the time by Mr L.M. Brew, with Mr Goodfellow, his farm manager. Billy Brighton and Bill Garnham are cutting seed kale, around 1955, with the help of modern engine power.

This hay-gathering scene was in the field opposite the Tally Ho! pub at Mettingham, on the Bungay to Beccles road, with the men taking a break and leaning on their pitch forks, or shouldering them. The year was around 1935.

Above: Mettingham was, and still is, largely a farming community. This is a typical farmyard scene in the Waveney Valley in 1949 with Mr Aldous driving the Fordson tractor, pulling a wagon of hay, at Prospect Farm, Mettingham. Mark Gooch can just be seen on the top of the load.

Right: This time the tractor is a Ferguson TVO, with John Reeve ploughing on Spring Field at Alder Farm, Mettingham, in 1953. The farm house is in the distance.

Above: Red House Farm at Mettingham won several prizes for the quality of its fruit. Here, owner Anthony Barkeley-Smith, seen in around 1952, holds one of the trophies, with three of his staff, from left to right: Teddy Fish; Rooney Hall and Freddie Harper.

Left: Doris Tilney needed a bike to get to her job as a bus conductress. Her base was Bungay and she was just setting off from home at The Cote, in High Road, Mettingham, to go to work, *c.* 1937.

Here is a country character once-familiar in the Waveney Valley – Fred Brock, of Mettingham, with the bowler hat he invariably wore and one of his dogs who was his constant companion. With him in this photograph, from the late 1930s, is Benny Brundle, aged about twelve.

This couple were married in the 1870s – the photograph was taken as they were celebrating their golden wedding anniversary – with the cake ready for cutting on the table beside them. They are Harry and Emily Hall, with members of their family. The photograph was taken opposite Vicarage Farm, Mettingham.

Almost certainly these two newly-weds were from farming families, so perhaps it was appropriate that their wedding photograph should have been taken in a sugar beet field, at Toll Bar, Mettingham. Martha Plummer is the bride and Harry Howlett the bridegroom – they were married on 30 September 1914. Their bridesmaids are in the photograph too and it gives a good insight into wedding fashions from an age when the First World War was just starting.

The fishing industry of the East Coast provided work for many people at its height and often they were from inland communities. Crew for Lowestoft trawlers were recruited as far afield as necessary and that was certainly the case here. The crew photographed in front of the wheelhouse of the *Lord Carnarvon*, berthed at Lowestoft fish docks, around 1925, included no fewer than five Mettingham men – three from the Bird family and two, Walter and Ephraim, from the Brighton family.

The Coronation of King George V in 1911 was royally celebrated throughout the land. This was the scene at Mettingham Hall, where the dining hall was elaborately decked out with bunting, flags, badges and trimmings and the tables were well laden. But it was clearly a 'men only' occasion – there are no women to be seen.

Above: This photograph shows an event at Mettingham in the 1930s, when a marquee was erected in the grounds of Mettingham Pavilion, in Low Road. Seated at the front in the centre are Mr J.H. Bezant and his wife. Mr Bezant was a Russian immigrant who settled in Mettingham and did much for the village and for Bungay, where he was the founding president of Bungay Town Football Club in 1925.

Opposite above: The annual fête in the grounds of Mettingham Hall was one that drew large crowds each year. The date here was around 1965, with Suzanne Hall (then a presenter with the BBC Regional Television) performing the opening. Beside her in the wheelchair is Mr Brew, the then owner of the hall.

Opposite below: Castle Farm, Mettingham, in the 1930s, with Mrs Gooch feeding the chickens beside the pond and Mr Gooch leading a horse, perhaps to pasture or stable after a hard days work.

St Peter's Hall, photographed in 1936. This ancient building dates in part from AD 950. In the sixteenth century architectural features from nearby Flixton Priory were added to it, the priory having been forced to close as a result of new legislation by Henry VIII. The building later became a farmhouse and is now the home of St Peter's Brewery, the deep-water borehole on the site provides excellent water for the many fine ales produced there.

Opposite above: The old Minster at South Elmham is thought to have been the residence of Almar, Bishop of East Anglia, in Saxon times. It is in the area known as 'the Saints' and the Deanery of South Elmham includes the other eight ancient parishes of St Michael, St Peter, St Margaret, St James, St Nicholas, St Cross, Flixton and Homersfield. This photograph is of the ruined west end of the Old Minster, *c.* 1935.

Opposite below: The east end of the Old Minster, South Elmham, *c.* 1935.

Other local titles published by Tempus

Bungay to Beccles
CHRIS AND TERRY REEVE

The Waveney Valley is one of the most picturesque areas of North Suffolk. This fascinating collection of over 200 photographs portrays the history of the towns of Bungay and Beccles and the area between them and how it has changed over the past one hundred years.

0 7524 1177 2

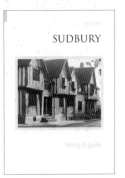

Sudbury History and Guide
BARRY WALL

The market town of Sudbury in Suffolk has long been considered an area of outstanding natural beauty. This fascinating insight into Sudbury's past details the town's history from Saxon times to the present day and includes a walking tour of the town.

0 7524 3317 2

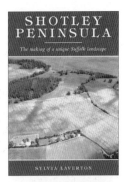

Shotley Peninsula The Making of a Unique Suffolk Landscape
SYLVIA LAVERTON

Blessed with better soil than most of Suffolk, from earliest times this peninsula in the south-east developed a particularly prosperous agricultural way of life. This is a book that will delight and inform anyone with a love of Suffolk, especially those with an interest in the county's Viking past.

0 7524 1937 4

Ipswich Town FC 100 Greats
TONY GARRETT

This fascinating insight into Ipswich Town Football Club details some of the greats who have played for the club over the years. It provides the reader with a fascinating insight into Town's sporting achievements since the club turned professional in 1936.

0 7524 2719 9

If you are interested in purchasing other books published by Tempus, or in case you have difficulty finding any Tempus books in your local bookshop, you can also place orders directly through our website

www.tempus-publishing.com